MW01688480

Face of a Gypsy

To Milla,
a life-long
cherished friend.
You're a blessing.
Eileen

Other publications by Eileen Curteis:

Risk (The King's Men, 1975)

Sojourner, Know Yourself (Sisters of Saint Ann, 1993)

Moving On (Ekstasis Editions, 1997)

Wind Daughter (Ekstasis Editions, 1998)

Dance of the Mystic Healer (Sisters of Saint Ann, 2001)
Includes a CD on which Sister Eileen recites her poems.

Dance of the Mystic Healer: Resurrection Songs (CD – 2002)

Soul Travel: A Roadway to Healing (Sisters of Saint Ann, 2002)
Includes a CD on which Sister Eileen recites her poems.

Reiki: A Spiritual Doorway To Natural Healing (Trafford, 2004)
Includes a CD on which Sister Eileen recites her poems – some being set to music.

Face of a Gypsy

Eileen Curteis

Ekstasis Editions

Library and Archives Canada Cataloguing in Publication

Curteis, Eileen, 1942-
Face of a gypsy / Eileen Curteis.

Poems
ISBN-13: 978-1-894800-92-1
ISBN-10: 1-894800-92-3

I. Title.

PS8555.U84F32 2007 C811'.54 C2007-906456-3

Cover Photo: Carol Porteous-Crawford

Published in 2007 by:
Ekstasis Editions Canada Ltd.
Box 8474, Main Postal Outlet
Victoria, B.C. V8W 3S1

Ekstasis Editions
Box 571
Banff, Alberta T1L 1H5

The Canada Council for the Arts since 1957 | Le Conseil des Arts du Canada depuis 1957

British Columbia Arts Council
Supported by the Province of British Columbia

Ekstasis Editions wishes to thank the following for their support of its publishing program: the Canada Council for the Arts, and the Province of British Columbia through the British Columbia Arts Council.
First edition. Printed in Canada.

For my living and deceased family
who have always affirmed me –
Tom, Lil, Chuck, Wendy, Carson, Jason, Melaney, Dorothy

and

For the Community of the Sisters of Saint Ann
who have allowed my gift to flourish

Contents

Seer, Poet, Healer: An Introduction to *Face Of A Gypsy*

When I first had the pleasure of meeting Sister Eileen Curteis through a mutual friend fourteen years ago, the bonding was immediate. Sister Eileen lives at Queenswood Centre in Victoria, B.C. She is a poet, artist, writer and a Reiki Master who leads workshops in this ancient eastern method of healing within a Christian context. Sister Eileen continues in the line of Thomas Merton and others who have integrated the wisdom of east and west in their lives and art. As Merton put it,

> I think we have now reached a stage (long overdue) of religious maturity at which it may be possible for someone to remain perfectly faithful to a Christian and Western (monastic) commitment, and yet to learn in depth from...a Buddhist discipline and experience.
> (*The Asian Journals*, 1975, xxiii)

For Sister Eileen, poetry is another art of spiritual healing or self-transformation through words and images. In her seven previous volumes she accompanies her poetry with her own spare sketches or carefully chosen photographic art that resonates with the text. Eileen's poetry contains things old and new, but all has been honed and transformed to a new precision of insight. The carefully chosen photographs that complement each poem enhance the reader's experience.

The collection contains precise, chiseled lyrics, cryptic wisdom sayings, moving elegies, and personal narratives of the soul in the throes of radical rebirth. Sister Eileen has delved deeply into her own experience of healing and regeneration, and into the riches of her Christian heritage to explore the unification of body, mind, soul and spirit that is the human quest.

The book opens with the figure of a seer in a cave, a kind of shamanic or sibyiline female in the cave of the body she has come to inhabit in a new way:

...she's a woman now
gone back to her origins
to see things we don't,
boots, bonnets, petticoats.
Her body knows what it was like
before she began falling back
into the womb of her mother.

The water was pure then,
and the rain came trickling down her face.
She loved everything,
the soft skin of humans, rabbits, birds, deer.
In the sweet scent of a rose
she could smell the essence of her being.
The sky was bluer in those days,
the sun brighter.
The universe was filled with light
and the Divinity was in her.
("A Seer Lives Inside The Hidden Hollow Of This Cave")

The poem reconstructs both pre-existence and eternal presence, so the poems that follow may trace the loss and partial recovery of this condition of complete openness.

The second poem then moves to the more ambivalent figure of the dark-eyed gypsy—the outcast, wanderer and nomad. By adopting the gypsy figure, Sister Eileen forwards concerns raised in her first seven volumes about itinerancy and outsideness. She then proceeds to interweave these figures of the seer and the gypsy throughout the collection to suggest their ultimate identity. Paradoxically, the outsider is the one who sees profoundly into the heart of things; the outsider is the true insider, the mystic of interiority:

Now that I have learned to accept
my own geography
nothing surprises me anymore—
("Dark-Eyed Face Of A Gypsy")

The poems are tied to several essential strands in the gospel narratives. They include: Jesus as wisdom figure (exiled Sophia of God), Jesus as prophet and social reformer, and Jesus as spiritual healer. By all accounts, Jesus lived an itinerant lifestyle that challenged the expectations of the religious and political establishments of his day. Eileen echoes his words from the gospel, "The Son of man has no place to lay his head," in her poem "I Found My Poppies Outside The System": "I am a winter bird/ that has no place/ to lay its head." The voice is often that of the plucky weed, trampled down but resilient. The speaker is "the despised and rejected" of Isaiah, flowering into an unstoppable fullness of being connected to the energy of resurrection:

> I saw my Healer dressing me
> in the same radiant cloth
> He wore
> three days after His burial.
> ("Behind The Eyes Of The Blind One A Sun Shone Through")

Yet the poems take us beyond the celebration of one person's healing into the realm of the "wounded healer," the once oppressed who becomes a transformer in her own right, extending Christly compassion for the outcast to children, the disabled, the aged—other outsiders made insiders:

> She knows who to invite
> giraffes, owls, rabbits, skunks,
> anyone
> without the pretense of a long tail.
>
> They would come just as they are
> lame, shabby, crippled, poor...
> ("Serenity")

Sister Eileen's poems are not only arresting in their concerns and symbolism, but finely wrought. I am entranced by her gift for the apparently bizarre, almost surreal image, the mixed metaphor that makes lucid poetic sense by delivering a jolt of recognition. These images are sometimes accompanied by a sense of violence and disturbance that is part of the process of healing. For example, in the poem "Growing Up":

> Then, as now, it saddens me
> how small things
> like the wishbone of a foetus
> get trampled over.

The most delightful metaphor of this sort is a domestic one in "A Woman Called Mary" where the Annunciation is like "the mop of God/...swishing down/ into the gutted earth."

The poems also insist on an almost Franciscan inclusion of small, meek things—flowers, birds, deer. Bird imagery, especially, abounds from "blind snowbirds" to "clothing eaten by birds." Sometimes the speaker addresses herself as a bird:

> ...it's time snowbird
> stopped abandoning her vehicle...
> ("Snowbird's New Song Exudes Joy")

Consider the lyric delicacy of bird imagery in

> All day
> a flutter of wings,
> all night
> a cradle of birds
> chirping in her womb.
>
> All earth
> a heaven to soar in.
> ("Child Of Ecstasy")

Face Of A Gypsy is finally about reclaiming the body, and the body's reclaiming of the soul and Spirit from which it has never really been separate. The book provides a gentle resistance to all that oppresses the emancipatory perspective, all that inhibits praise:

...it comes slowly this rejoicing
the day after the morning of nothing before.
("Springtime Happenings Birthing Joy Into Us")

Yet Eileen's deep song emerges from what Merton calls in *Conjectures of a Guilty Bystander,* the "point vierge," the nothingness of almost total diminishment and extinction, a kind of crucifixion or "dark night of the soul." By dancing through the death of the self, the poems lead us into the business of resurrection as a daily practice. The poems suggest that each of us is called at some level to be a mystic and a healer—of ourselves, each other and the world—re-enacting the journey of Christ:

Her hand is on the latch of her soul.
The door she opens goes inward.
("Mysterious Eyes Of A Well Travelled Woman")

Dr. Susan McCaslin
Instructor of English
Douglas College, New Westminster, B.C.
August 31, 2006.

A Seer Lives Inside The Hidden Hollow Of This Cave

I've travelled far into the unusual
but never have I seen anything so strange
as this seer in a cave
sitting still in a chair bending backwards
when she wants to go forward.

Going in opposite directions to ours
she could be a dumb pigeon
paddling her way home
or more likely
a young girl with an ancient existence
humming her song into the trees.

Guided by the Spirit of an eagle
she's a woman now
gone back to her origins
to see things we don't,
boots, bonnets, petticoats.
Her body knows what it was like
before she began falling back
into the womb of her mother.

The water was pure then,
and the rain came trickling down her face.
She loved everything
the soft skin of humans, rabbits, birds, deer.
In the sweet scent of a rose
she could smell the essence of her being.
The sky was bluer in those days, the sun brighter.
The universe was filled with light
and the Divinity was in her.

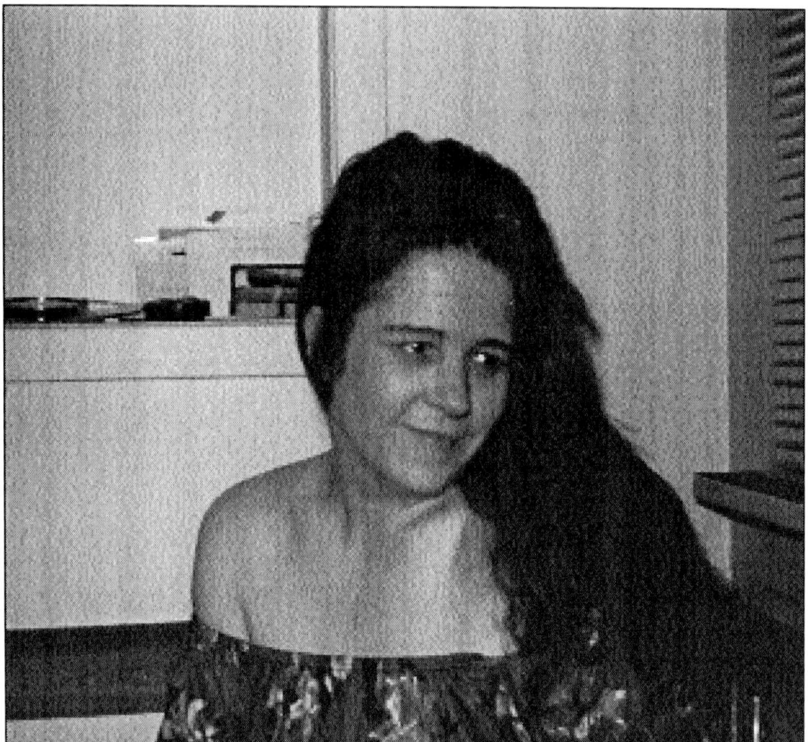

Dark-Eyed Face Of A Gypsy

Now that I have learned to accept
my own geography
nothing surprises me anymore –
    fresh cream
    on a sour potato
    spoiled hamburger
    on a rotten egg –
what does it matter
when the ingredients are you?

Are not each of us
    born
    raised
    chosen
but how many would disclose
the vain wrinkle
in our weak world?

And how many
when the time comes
could look in a mirror and say:
    "I see you, face of a gypsy,
    dark eyes
    black
    as an untamed stallion
    peering out at me,
    peering out at you,
    I see you, face of a gypsy."

Behind The Eyes Of The Blind One
A Sun Shone Through

The Voice came toward me,
"Blind one with the darkened eyes
let me lead you"
and I in answer said:
"Even if you throw my clothes away
to be eaten by the birds
I will let you lead me!"

Sitting on the sharp edge of a craggy cliff
I had spent my entire life-time
trying to be happy
but now it felt like the black hole of a pit
had torn the skin away from my smile.

I could have ended my journey here
had not a strange, beautiful Hand
lifted the veil from my unseeing eyes
telling me
blindness was the cataract
I walked into.

Under the cloud
a sun came rolling in
and for the first time
I saw my Healer dressing me
in the same radiant cloth He wore
three days after His burial.

The Wisdom Of Torn Skirts

Roots in my cellar
and more roots
enough to cover me
from the shame of living here
but I am not ashamed.

Fighting for life
I've gone down under the brambles
held love like a lily
seen terror
the poisoned blackberry
cut me up like a thorn
cut me down like a tree.

I've seen death on the highway
flown into her like a blind bird.
Driving down wrong roads
in search of the right shore
for a girl to walk on
I've crossed over the bridge
called ugly
to embrace the goodness in me.

My torn skirts
have aged me considerably.

Snowbird's New Song Exudes Joy

Grown cold
as a shivering sun
it's time snowbird
stopped abandoning her vehicle.

Limbs frozen
below zero temperatures
she knows the road alright
but a song
smothered in a blanket
is getting her nowhere.

She wants music
real music
like a symphony orchestra
to play with.

Already she feels lighter.

Autumn bursts its seeds
and she laughs
at the yellow face of a dandelion
chasing her up a winter hill.

Playful,
this dumb weed
scooting around the earth
has given more joy
to her silent tongue
than a bear hibernating
ever could.

Spinner's Web

If you let it
a cranky crow
can lead you to insanity
its black beak
cawing the life out of you.

It's no different
than junk mail piled high
you've got to wade through it
and stop blaming the postman
when it's yourself
delivering the clutter.

If you think sainthood means
hanging yourself on a rope
burning the skin off your fingers
you've got it all wrong.
It's inane the way you suffer.

A motorcycle going berserk
on the highway
could just as easily be you
rushing around making yourself sick.
You're drinking poison
one more tablespoon
and you'll be in the grave
writing your eulogy.

There are other options, you know,
a spider spinning a web
could be the true prophet
and so could you.

Ask yourself:
Is not complexity
the cloth of your own weaving
the burdensome knot
of the strand you tie?
In the loom of your heart
melody is a simple thread
woven out of the Spinner's yarn
the soft yoke of the breeze you lean on.

Warming My Body, Warming My Soul

For years people were saying –
you heat nothing.
Nothing heats you.
You are fire without fire,
flame without flame,
and they were right
nothing did heat me
in a world where cold
was growing colder than cold.

January went down
as the worst winter on record.
People were moving in then, by hordes
and I had already left the premises,
a polar bear of sorts
disoriented as to north.

Travelling abroad
I wondered if it was I
wearing the overshoes of a teddy bear
or someone else
looking for the land of the sun?

Wherever I went
I could feel my soft, white fur.
It was long and different from the others.
Travelling here, travelling there,
it was my own body
I got warmed by.

Child Of Ecstasy

Guzzling milk from mother's breast
no wonder this child swirls
like a hoop in the heart.

Stars, slurping down her throat,
she drinks in everything.
Fireflies, dancing on the tongue,
she swallows them whole.
Flowers, perfuming the air,
her nostrils fall into them.
Oceans, roaring in her ear,
she sprinkles them
with the salt of her soul.
Peacocks, flaring their tails to the sky,
she names them rainbow
after her.

All day
a flutter of wings,
all night
a cradle of birds
chirping in her womb.

All earth
a heaven to soar in!

Growing Up

Some animals are strange
but, then,
who knows what strange really is?
My mother used to say
a cat is strange
but when you're a kitten
you don't look on it that way.

As much as I hate to admit it
I guess growing up
was something of an oddity.
People in the neighbourhood said
I was the perfect little girl
with the perfect little smile.
Sitting on a high chair
you could have spotted me anywhere
broken, but growing up
like an indestructible toy.

Then, as now, it saddens me
how small things
like the wishbone of a foetus
get trampled over.

Dancing To New Rhythms, Lost Girls Find Their Woman Souls Young Again

Pushed down,
fallen,
under the weight of a mountain
sometimes North American girls
born into North American families
don't make it.

Their mothers say,
"Now dear,
you have everything
a third world child doesn't –
food, clothes, toys, games, money,
bracelets, earrings, necklaces –
everything a third world child doesn't!"

"Yes, mommy,"
they say,
"cock-a-doodle-doo!"
and go to bed hungry
as a chewed up rooster.

You can't fool these girls!
They know
when a chocolate
turning over in its sleep
isn't real.
Insipid
as day old phlegm
in the throat,
there is no substitute
for love
when it goes down
like a sugarless candy.

Were you to ask these girls,
“What is a heart?”
they would cry,
“a bell clanging
homesick
for its mother!”

Hankering for Love
they could be the best girls
in the world
blowing their lungs out
of a bugle
and still not be heard.

Driving uphill
into the new millennium
you may think there is no hope
for small girls on a scooter
grown big enough
to have the mouth of God in them
but look again.

Dancing sure-footed
you’ll not find them tiptoeing
around a naked tree in winter.

As sure as God is
they’ll come stomping
out of the kitchen
into a home
whose walls
can no longer confine them.

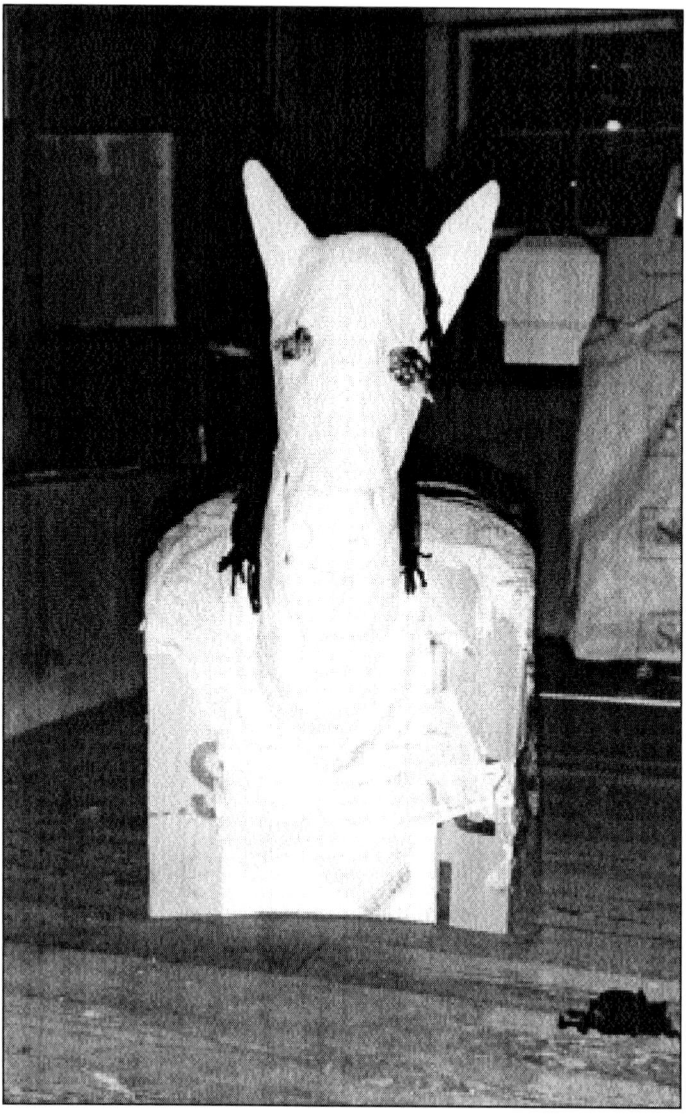

Wooden Horse Becomes Real

Wanting to help, I wept,
oh, how I wept
but the wooden horse without feeling
could not hear.

Punctured by life
she lay still
in her bed of straw
a dark-eyed, loveable creature.

Strapped down
held in
by too many reins
she saw what death could do.

Tears came
and the lost animal
went clomping in them
clomping, clomping.

Each time she fell
or cut a hoof
her flesh
became like stigmata.

Swallowing the night air
some say
her blood ran down the sap of a tree.
Others heard a soft sound
on the far side of the north wind.
Perhaps a small girl playing a flute
or a pony neighing her way home.

I Found My Poppies Outside The System

I am a winter bird
that has no place
to lay its head.
I am winter all over
with a song in my heart
and no one to hear.
I sit on people's windows
pecking
at their closed-inness.
I sing
far beyond my strength
for the day
when they shall hear
and I will be gone.

Migrating south
I could be as present as your finger is
or as anonymous as my name has become.
A stranger at school today
nobody sees
the cavity called loneliness
in the desk where I sit.
Like a sliver of wood
I am too small
to be seen by anyone.
I have gone to this school
for twelve years now,
but I am too small
to be seen by anyone.

At university
I play the game called funeral.
Nobody attends the ceremony.
Only my books do.
Years later,
like sunshine
spurting out
from under the closed lid
of a coffin,
I kiss that stupid kid
in a wastebasket
better.

I'm a degreed person
who found her poppies
outside the system.

The Past Is Past Lara

Fine features
carved into a stone,
it was Lara's face
that etched me in,
so many Lara's
so many knots
tied up in a string,
a pain here
a canker there,
but why go on being Lara?

It's not good
putting your face
in an empty bucket, Lara.
The past is past.
Gone, finished,
like white frost
frozen
on the stump of a tree.

Change your name, Lara,
and with it
the grey jacket
zippered into your skin.

Freshen up a little
be a bubble
bouncing on a ball
or try dancing barefoot
on a flattened shoe.

You can do it, Lara,
but remember
nothing is permanent
so why forecast anything.

Bad weather spelled backwards
in Africa
could be clear day
in America.

Orange Sun At My Window

Cheryl, orange sun at my window,
some of us get tipped over
by the smudge of life early
and go down the way of a fish
after spawning,
but we don't stay there.

Like you, Cheryl, we sail on
with our masts up
and, so, for your bravery
I would like to give you
something tender
soft yams in the fall
or hummingbirds in the spring.

I'll put up a sign on the fence
marked Cheryl,
year of the lilac,
and with a purple bloom
I'll cover your sweet, strong face
with the incense of this summer air.

Perennial plant at my window
you'll always be Cheryl to me.
Even in winter
when the blizzards come
I'll stoke the fire
and name the season after you.

A Flute Player's Joy

Her disfigured face
is gnarled like an oak
but on the south side
of her window
it's a gala of spring.

Behind the closed curtain
she hears the song of a bird
flapping its wings open.
It could be herself
sipping the last juice of winter.

In her new home, bitter wood is sweet
drab music, ethereal.
If joy could be measured
by the soft strain of a flute
hers would be incomparable.

You might think she's invincible
and, yet,
when the rain comes pouncing
through the trees
she tastes every morsel of it.

If you push her aside
or grind her up like a rock
she'll not crumble
under any storm.

In the strongest wind
she'll come out singing.

Home Of The Non Judgemental

Anything goes in this clearing –
    mountains, prairies, hills,
    children with rickets
    old men with rabies
    sunlight on a crocus
    moonlight on a canary
    and you
    girl tiger
    prostrate
    on your mother's knee.

Nobody cringes at anybody here –
    cat snores
    baby coos
    dog licks cat
    cat licks dog
    dog licks baby
    cat barks
    dog mews
    baby coos.

It doesn't matter who you are –
    awake or asleep
    we lie down together
    counting
    not heads
   but memories,
   how we came to be here.

Springtime Happenings Birthing Joy Into Us

Each has her time for the smothered air
when the light goes out
when the glimmer is gone
when the only thing left
is to hope there might be a hope.

Surprisingly enough
that's the way
the barren tree does it too,
uncomely for awhile
like the first burst of life anywhere.

The child coming into our world
the parent leaving us
it comes slowly this rejoicing
the day after the morning of nothing before.

Friendship

Some say friends are a matter of taste
and I guess I would have to agree.
In an orchard
each fruit has its distinct flavour:
peach, pear, apricot, plum.
And so it is,
in the field of a person's friendship.

Not everyone flocks to the same tree
at the same time
and yet,
there is enough fruit for everyone.

Life goes on
and there is no end to its vastness.
People come and people go.
Today
it's hemlock, cedar, pine cone, fir.
Tomorrow
there's no knowing
where the scent will come from.

Ocean Survivor Becomes Human

The crashing, crushing power of these waves
where were they then, where are they now
and were you above water or below it
when the depletion came?

Fine to say,
"wear me down like a rock"
but who wants to get worn down that way?
And when you get covered
by the restless eddy of an ocean
do you say,
"let me die swallowing my own water,"
or do you come up floating on the other side?

Be careful how you survive
the obsolete.
You could end up empty
draining the ocean like a tub.
Too much
too little of anything
is dangerous.

Picture yourself a whale
lapping up the land
one more bite
and the world would collapse over you.

Habitats vary,
an otter in a pub
a porpoise in a tub.
Absurdity
is what makes us human.

A New Future Free From Your Cancerous Ways

How can you say sugar is sweet
when you give me these spineless jelly beans?
It's like saying,
        "keep me in the locked cupboard
        of your superficiality
        and I will grow forever,"
but who wants that?

The last time I loved you
was like sucking acid
from a lemon
when I knew very well you didn't care for me.
Ignoring me the way you do
flat down, face into the wall,
is like falling into a room I can't get out of,
an insipid kind of shallow
you never quite get used to.

Just yesterday you did it again.
You said you loved me
but what kind of a pretender are you?
I can't go on accepting your love
as something convenient.
Convenient is why I am eating
the leather skin of a berry.
Convenient is you the day after a love affair
giving me the bread
after it sticks to the roof of your mouth.
Convenient is no longer convenient!

Grass Girl Quietly Jubilant Over The Garden Within

I am a cocoon that flies by night.
I live in the white house next door to you
but you do not know me.
Without food, without bone,
my tongue like a dog
hangs dry.

Lodged in the rusty hinge
of your closed door
I do not open easily.
My tin heart cries
but there are no tears.

Travelling
in my frigid air
there is no room
inside my house, inside my walls.
There is no room for me or anyone.

Night passes.
A Visitor comes
descending
like a white dove.
My cocoon bursts, my flower opens.
I rise out of the bed I am in.
My limbs rise with me.

Fragile
as green grass
swaying in the wind,
I run through the field with You.

Like a bent post
my body leans against You.
Old, tired hungry ghost
rises out of me.

You love me
and I let myself be loved.
Touching me with your Hand
a warm sun fills me.
I see now
how You garden in me.

Autumn Burial

At this funeral
pride
is the dandelion puffball
being blown away.

Spring

I cannot run fast enough to find her.
I cannot run fast enough!
When I hold her
she's intangible as the wind
and delicate as the rain.
She comes softly
like a whisper in the trees
softly, softly, softly.
She has no hair, no hands, no feet.
Her home is in the air
and nothing is as fragrant!

Open World

Yes
I was driven
by the timid voice
of a frail bloom,
but now I say,
  "small girl
   open the gate wide
   fling yourself upward,"
not because
I am afraid to fall
but because
I want more out of life
than standing crooked
on the broken rung
of a ladder.

In the same way
if a boulder flattens me
I get up from under it
and if I have any sense at all
I don't tell the rock
to lie down over me
once I have my feet
on the ground.

Instead,
I climb out
of the closed world I was in
and let myself be
ten, twenty feet taller
or whatever the height
out there is.

Second Calling

When He calls a second time
hasten to listen
and if it is you He is beckoning
let not your face be hidden
but go as wings would have you go
stretching forth your hand
your right hand to meet Him.

And if His voice
be in the wind you hear
let Love lead you.

Allow nothing to deter you
no breeze, no storm, no faulty motion
but if for whatever reason
the air be contrary
let it be contrary.

If you want the best
imagine it –
new eyes
going through a narrow door
where the Light comes streaming through.

Shifting horizons,
you get to see the sun
on the other side.

A Woman Called Mary

The sky wept
and out of it the mop of God
came swishing down
into the gutted earth.
It was a day of worship, a great day,
when the world was full of God
and God was full of the world.

On that day, God visited the earth and said:
"Let there be moisture, enough of it
to wash you with the cleanliness of snow"
and what God said, God did.
God saw everywhere what needed to be seen
and God went where God needed to go.

First, God saw the tiny knitted suit of an infant
and God said, "Let my life grow
into the body of a woman"
and what God said, God did.
From then on God's eyes rested on a maiden.
She was young, brave and beautiful.

One day God lay down beside her.
Seven days and seven nights
God sat there and rested.
On the eighth day,
unbeknown to the world,
God kissed the petal of a daisy
and named her Mary.
On that day, Mary was with Child.

If Only

If only I could put a smile
    on the face of the squashed cricket
    she'd come out lilting this time.
If only I could put a star
    on the other side of a rain cloud
    no one would consume me.
If only with sweet music
    I could quiet the mother
    who shuts out the racket of her baby.
If only I could gather the garbage
    and put out a banquet of clean food
    when the hungry come.
If only I could put soft wool
    over your coarse skin
    I would not snore over you.
If only the mailman would leave me
    with something other than emptiness
    on the far end of a blank page.
If only my small home in the city
    would welcome every wheelchair
    when it came in.
If only I lived in a perfect world
    where nobody spilt coffee on anyone
    unless they had to.
If only I could think quickly
    I'd not be
    the last person to put my hand up.
If only mother lived
    when the plane crashed
    I could have taken her to the movie.
If only my dog would dry her nose
    before she licks me
    I would like her better.

If only the doctor
    could make me stay well
    I wouldn't get sick.
If only I could run a race
    and not always be
    the one that comes out losing.
If only I could be queen
    for a day
    and wear my crown into eternity.

So Much To Hope For With Your Hand In Mine

I am not usually broken
but when I am
I need you
like wax in a candle
to melt into me.
With your hand in mine
I need you to say:
    "I who have fallen
    out of gaiety before
    can embrace it again."

As much
as I should know
I am loveable
sometimes I don't.
That's why
the link of your arm
in mine
has something to say
to all of us in desperation.

Something about
how we can't always be
on top of the stairs
and yet,
if somebody hopes in us
there's no saying
how high we will climb.

Upright Trees

No water
nothing in the barren soil
to lure her
she goes into dark places
puts forth tendrils over the dry land
and in the dead garden sprouts life
out of a withered bean.

She replenishes the earth
puts life back into drab things.
To the stale stream, she gives drink,
to the dry dust, moisture
and those in distress
she likens to trees
that shall stand upright.

Follow The Road That Befriends You

Silence these harsh words
on the sharp blade of a tongue
sticking into you, sticking into me
sticking into everyone.
Silence all gossipers
all those who snub out the good
from another.
Silence them.
Silence the wicked, the fraud, the evil
the trickery in those eyes.
Silence them.
Silence all haughty looks
all hard faces with their damaging smiles.
Silence them.
The unkind, the mean, the narrow, the small
silence all that we are prisoner to.
Silence the mother who strikes her child
because the father says to.
Silence her.
Silence that two-faced lady
innocent child that she isn't;
that man with the closed lid
concealing only half truths
silence him.
Silence all in all.
Even your own funny creature in the mirror
silence her.
At all times befriend the world
let the world befriend you
but above all be wary of the devil dozing
he could be sleeping
next to you.

Serenity

is a cat worth celebrating,
a tabby cat
on the horizon
inviting true lizards to her party,
not the barbarian kind
who lick the icing from your cake.

She knows who to invite
giraffes, owls, rabbits, skunks,
anyone
without the pretense of a long tail.

They would come just as they are
lame, shabby, crippled, poor,
each bringing some small gift
for the other.

Hearts burning
like chopped wood on the fire
they would sit there for days
polite animals, content
to have the golden
soft foot of dusk
descend upon them.

Sometimes you would swear
they were human –
intelligent eyes
piercing through the sham
of another day.

Recovery

Standing before you
in a cold room
where love is vacant
you are where I am not.

In this kind of graveyard,
past the wilderness
on the other side
of your granite eyes
I will not mourn
a root gone dead.

I'll just say
in some dusty corner
hanging on the dank face
of a cobweb
you will not find me.

Changing Silhouettes

In my silhouette I see a woman
cutting holes
through other people's garments,
including mine.
Silk, cotton, corduroy, whatever the cloth,
she's hemming it the wrong way.
In her company
the frayed dress gets frayer
trousers end up at the knees
and skirts once straight hang crooked.

Scissors, needles, pins,
it's time she changed her wardrobe.
Take a look at her mind.
It's like fabric
she takes a match to
and worse than that
it burns her body down.

Smearing ashes over a graveyard
is not a bad thing
when it produces the life it came for.
You may think you know this woman,
but not really.

The last time she came out of a dark cupboard
wearing red
you saw the marred face of a stranger
and yet, she bore the grace of a woman
who knew herself.

Morning Awakening

Silent moon
yawning boredom to the night,
my doctor's hand flops into insomnia
the way my prescription does.

Mother consoles me
hot milk, "warm jammies,"
says sleep comes when the stars vanish
and it's dark out.

Teacher says
sleep, like intelligence,
is the black blind
you pull down at night.

My pastor thinks
bad girls go to bed
with their eyes open
and none of them are right.

Insomnia is insomnia
a wrinkled nightgown
in a tangled sheet
I must get out of.

Sleepless, but wakened
by a mauve bird in summer wind
I slide into morning this way.

Hair, strangled in a bow,
I no longer need to be perfect
to make the day right.

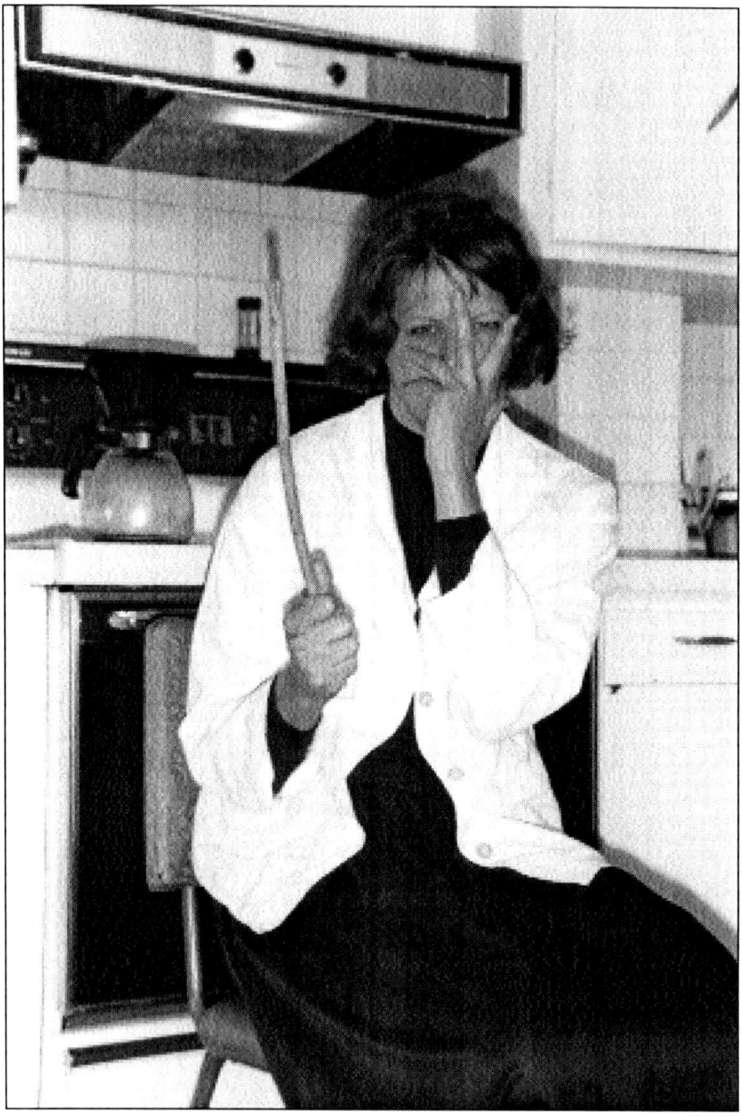

Contradictions

Behind the t.v.
your face
is the newspaper
blocking my view.

Ignoring me
is like putting a hollow tube
in your deaf ear.

Can you hear me?

What I want
is not thin air
tiptoeing around my kitchen
but you to hold.

It's misleading isn't it
the way we cover our cloth faces
with a dangle of hair?
And that permanent smile we wear
sometimes I would like to take a stick to it!

Chiselled

Before you came
there was so much emptiness
inside the glass cage of my tottering house
statues wanting to be made out of stone
and then,
fear the Chisler would come.

And you did come
saw, hammer and nail
into the heart of a brittle bone
that ran far from you!
Each time you came
I showed you the chipped part
of a hand or leg
or the flattened part of my body
I wanted to hide under.
Sometimes I wore something different
to shelter me
red hat, yellow dress,
whatever it was
you always said I looked best
in the clothing of a naked seamstress.

Stripping me was never easy,
the skin stuck out all over,
but gradually I became myself
and hid nothing from you.
One day I chided you and said,
"I hate the hard hand of a cruel Carver,"
but underneath it all
I grew to love you.

Portrait of a Soul

I know you
though you speak
but little of yourself.
Sorrow
has silenced you
has made you gentle
and radiant.
Words –
they are no longer necessary.
I have only to look in your eyes.

Mother's Face Gone Radiant

Ice, winter ice,
it's not what I intended
and yet the wall was there
keeping me from you.

On the other side
of the fence
my heart went roaming.
I pretended not to see you.

I could have been
a cat, a dog, a mouse
busily chasing my tail.

Today, I'm human –
out there in the desolate snow
crushing weeds from my past.

Far off in the distance
I see the radiant face
of an old woman
I have forgotten to love.

Like the sweet scent of lilac
I come close enough to touch
and hold her in my hands.

A Tribute to Lil

First of all, the eyes
blue enough to indulge in,
the ones your children inherited.

Gazing at you now
is like opening a book
wrinkled in time
knowing you as you were –
pure face
no cloud could hide,
no stone could shatter.

As gentle as you were,
you rode through life
with the spirit of a stallion
and carried your duality well.

Washing the dishes, scrubbing the floors,
putting meals on the table
you saw beauty in the ordinary
and we loved you for it.

I think God must have been proud of you
when the mouth of the blue sky opened
and you came sailing into our lives
not to charm, but to love us.

Perhaps that's the miracle of motherhood.
You came like a beautiful clock
ticking your way into us.

You were just an ordinary mom
lighting a lamp in dark places,
and now, dear mother of ninety-eight,
even if you tried to hide your brightness
behind an eclipse of the moon
we would still find you shining.

Dear splendid butterfly on bended wing
we will not hold you back
from your soaring
when the time comes.

Instead,
we'll gather the lilies,
and the scent of your face
will be on them
fresh, as if you never had gone into hiding.

Even In Death Dad's Love Will Heal

Black,
colour of a torn up tulip,
stick it on your father's face
until the eyes become indelible
as yours.

Genealogy has it
the daughter inherits
the look of her father.
One glance from these navy eyes
and she has the uncanny ability
to light up the dark corners
of a dim room.

They are so much alike,
father and daughter.
A small girl
somersaulting down a hill
she exudes humour
as freely as he does
only sometimes
she catches him playing
with dust balls in the thermos
as if there was something wrong
with growing old
something irreversible
as bad breath.

She can't stop loving this man
he's the only dad she has
and she'd do anything to keep him forever
relinquish calendars
turn clocks backward

put him in her pocket
with a warm blanket marked
eternal daddy.

She remembers him as he was
huge heart size of an ocean
forty years a school principal
loved, honoured, respected,
friend of children, parents
this beautiful man
falling off a pedestal
into a pit called no more
and she wants to save him.

Daddy's girl,
mischievous monkey,
they could be twins
in the same buggy
identical shoe laces
each going their separate way
he on one continent
she on another.

Long after he's gone
she'll remember her tiny hand in his
the big finger over the little one
tracing the word love
down the side of her cheek.

More Precious Than A Timid Deer

We cherish those people
who cross our hearts
with the footprints of love.
My brother is one of those people.

I had always known and loved him
but for some strange reason
I loved him more that winter
than any other.

He called me by my name.
"Crushed snowdrop," he said,
"more precious than a timid deer,
you are loveable as anyone,"
and with that the growth began.

That winter
for whatever reason
he held me
as if I never had been held,
loved me
as if I never had been loved.
My brother.

Your Eyes Will See

Blind eye
in a permanent fog
I walk out of
that's me
at the turn of the century.

Picture me now –
a staggering lily
wanting to stand upright
or a blank page
longing to be written on.

Coming of age is like that:
you want to be the clean Voice
of God
blowing the dust out of the trees
but you're not there yet.

More than anything
you want to step over the edge
of being afraid
of nothing
and even though
you have never entered this abyss
you can feel it coming.

Funky Girl
Smelling the Funky Flowers

It might be true
we're flourishing
as well as anybody
but sometimes
we're like weed and bramble
growing together.

Nobody says
we shouldn't be there
and, so,
we go on existing
not knowing
there's a better garden
elsewhere.

Sometimes
that's what getting
dug up means.
You end up
in different soil.

Trees, bushes, flowers, people,
everything takes on
a new savour,
and what you get
is a taste
distinctively your own.

Snowdrops

Will they believe me
if I say:
    "Forget the fertilizer
    snowdrops
    are in the torn sprout
    of your forgotten potato."

Or will they
with their shovels to the earth
reply:
    "Sick dirt
    nobody can make us grow.
    We die with our roots up."

And they are right.
They do die.
Resurrection
is a plant of the future
a worm with a flower in it.

Where they are
you have been,
grovelling
one foot
on the metallic chain of a pedal
going nowhere with the seasons,
the other
reviving underground
in the clay of an unknown climate
extinct, perhaps,
to those who have not dug far enough.

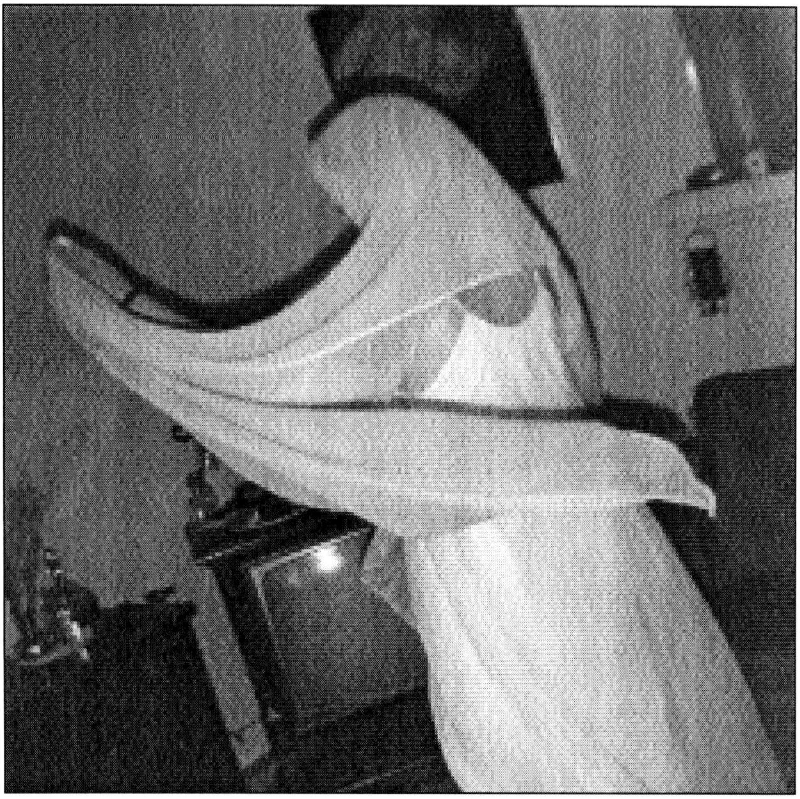

Sleep-Walker

In some societies
you don't dream
of being a sleep-walker
you just are.

People greet you with:
        Carry your own sled
        to the big city
        where the igloos are!
                        or
        What's that –
        a face under your hood?

Knowing your identity
is one thing
but having it smashed
into the ground
is not what you came for.

You could be a beggar
sporting the clothes of Jesus
and they'd still be putting
a shawl over you.

Thick fog
it's not you who's wearing the veil
but they who fail to see.

Mysterious Eyes of a Well Travelled Woman

Coat, gloves, scarves,
is there any safety in these
when you are your own worst iceberg?
Why not build a fire indoors
to save you
from this frozen climate?

Wood, logs, paper,
what good are these
unless you risk
the loss of your own soul?
And where will you find yourself
if not in the fuel
of your burnt clothing?

What's happening to you is no different
than the story of magnanimous Jesus
who catches his foot on a railway track
and the train goes ploughing through him.

Face it
Santa Claus
won't be coming down your chimney
this year
but the thud of an axe will.

Falling off the edge of a cliff
you might say
half your life is over.
Put an X on it, and know,
on a scale of one to ten
oblivion
is not a bad place to be.

Putting it another way
the dictionary definition of well travelled
could mean a woman
standing on a secluded street in Paris
waiting to be famous
but you know otherwise.
Her hand is on the latch of her soul.
The door she opens goes inward.

Acknowledgements:

Some of these poems have appeared in the following books, periodicals, journals and newspapers: *The Open Window, No Love Lost II, Vox Feminarum, The Victoria Naturalist, Canadian Woman Studies, paperplates, Grail, Prairie Messenger, Island Catholic News, L'Antenne, Forward In The Spirit, The Open Window* and *No Love Lost II.*

I would like to thank Susan McCaslin for editing my book, for writing the wonderful introduction and for her continuing friendship and belief in me as a poet. I am also grateful to my publisher, Richard Olafson, for his ongoing support, to those who read and wrote endorsements for my book and to my many friends who contributed their photography.

Photography acknowledgements:

A Seer Lives Inside The Hidden Hollow
Of This Cave - J. Douglas Porteous
Dark-Eyed Face Of A Gypsy - Morey Dupray
Behind The Eyes Of the Blind One A
Sun Shone Through - Jason Curteis
Snowbird's New Song Exudes Joy - Suzanne Derricks
Warming My Body, Warming My Soul - Helen Normandeau, O.S.U.
Child Of Ecstasy - Morey Dupray
Growing Up - Jances Moody-Stuart
Wooden Horse Becomes Real - Virginia Surina
I Found My Poppies Outside The System - Carol Porteous-Crawford
The Past Is Past Lara - Helen Normandeau, O.S.U.
Orange Sun At My Window - Lonnie Murphy
A Flute Player's Joy – Kevin Norman
Home Of The Non Judgemental - Suzanne Derricks
Ocean Survivor Becomes Human - Theresa van Schaik
Grass Girl Quietly Jubilant Over The Garden Within - Jason Curteis
Autumn Burial - Jason Curteis
Spring - Carol Porteous-Crawford

Second Calling - Helen Normandeau, O.S.U.
So Much To Hope For With Your Hand In Mine - Jason Curteis
Upright Trees - Joyce Harpell
Follow The Road That Befriends You - Lawrence De Mong
Serenity - Theresa van Schaik
Recovery - Jason Curteis
Changing Silhouettes - Jason Curteis
Morning Awakening - Peter Gubbels
Contradictions - Lonnie Murphy
Chiselled - Kathleen Kler
Mother's Face Gone Radiant – Alison DeCotiis
Even In Death Dad's Love Will Heal - Chuck Curteis
More Precious Than A Timid Deer - Chuck Curteis
Your Eyes Will See - Pamela Hodges
Funky Girl Smelling The Funky Flowers - Carol Porteous-Crawford
Snowdrops - Peter Gubbels
Sleep Walker - Morey Dupray
Mysterious Eyes of a Well-Travelled Woman - Richard Olafson

Attempts have been made to locate the photographers but unfortunately they remain unknown:

The Wisdom Of Torn Skirts
Spinner's Web
Springtime Happenings Birthing Joy Into Us
Friendship
A New Future Free From Your Cancerous Ways
Open World
A Woman Called Mary
Portrait Of A Soul
A Tribute To Lil